THE FOURTH WAVE

© 2014–2019 Jennifer Armbrust

All rights reserved. No part of this book may be reproduced, stored in a retrieval system, or transmitted in any form or by any means, electronic, mechanical, photocopying, recording or otherwise without the prior permission of the publisher.

Published by The Fourth Wave
P.O. Box 422, Carpinteria, CA 93014
thefourthwaveisfeminine.com

An earlier version of this book was published as a PDF in 2014.

Design: Jennifer Armbrust

ISBN: 978 1 7336353 1 8

Distributed by Sister
sister.is

10 9 8 7 6 5 4 3 2 1

THE BUSINESS BIRTHING HANDBOOK

A THEORY OF TRIMESTERS

JENNIFER ARMBRUST

IT'S ARCHETYPAL · 7
HOW TO USE THIS HANDBOOK · 14
YOU ARE NOT YOUR BUSINESS · 17

THE GESTATIONAL STAGES

CONCEPTION
23

VISIONING
FIRST TRIMESTER · 35

ENGINEERING
SECOND TRIMESTER · 43

ACTUALIZATION
THIRD TRIMESTER · 53

NOTES · 64

BIRTHING A BUSINESS IS AN ARCHE-TYPAL PROCESS

IT'S ARCHETYPAL

Our mission at Sister is to help you build a beautiful, thriving business that embodies your values and to infuse your entrepreneurial journey with ease and enjoyment. Birthing a business is an archetypal process. Understanding that process (and where you are in it) will help you work with more flow and less overwhelm. It will also save you money and time, in the long run.

I have been a serial entrepreneur since 2002 and a business consultant since 2012. I'm the founder and director of Sister and the principal of Feminist Business School. My academic training is in Critical Theory, including feminist theory, political economy, and critical race theory. My work with Sister largely involves translating my experiential wisdom and academic scholarship into workable tools for entrepreneurs who want to bring feminist principles into their business practices.

A few years ago, I began playing with pregnancy as an analogy for birthing a business when my advisor, Liliana Barzola, suggested that a business is like a child. With some quick internet research, I was tickled to discover that the process of birthing a business bears a tidy correlation with the phases of prenatal development. I promptly wrote a short essay, *The Trimester Theory*, outlining the three sequential stages of business gestation—*Visioning, Engineering,* and *Actualization*—

and drawing parallels to the trimesters of fetal development.

As I began using this framework with some of my consulting clients, I discovered that I had neglected an essential part of the birthing process, the initiation stage—*Conception!* Some women felt a deep desire to bring a new enterprise into the world but didn't know what type of business they wanted to create, exactly. I realized it was impossible to undertake *Visioning* until they had conceived of their idea, until they had a clear *concept*. I expanded the framework to include the *Conception* stage and added some guiding questions for each stage. The yield is this Handbook.

The primary purpose of this tidy tome is to guide you through the archetypal process of bringing your business idea to life and to convey to you the immense value of the often-overlooked, more feminine stages: *Conception* and *Visioning*. If you are a new entrepreneur, most advisors will direct you to write a business plan. But so much magic is missed when you rush into devising a plan without taking the time to clarify your concept and flesh out your vision.

In my years of teaching and consulting, I've discovered that both new and seasoned entrepreneurs are prone to rushing into *Engineering* their business. *Engineering* is the stage where you write your business plan and devise the systems, structures, and day-to-day operations for your company. It's a visible, active stage of business development — you and everyone around you can see that you are working hard on your business. But, *Engineering* correlates with the second trimester of development, not the first. When you rush into *doing* you deny the radical power of your imagination and the wisdom of your intuition. In your quest to make your work visible (and therefore, valid) to the outside world, you will abandon the feminine parts of the process and the feminine parts of yourself.

As I wrote in my first book, *Proposals for the Feminine Economy,* part of the project of feminist entrepreneurship is a reimagining of work that honors pleasure, ease, abundance, introspection, interdependency, intuition, and invisible labor. Our collective obsession with productivity, efficiency, metrics, and the glorification of overworking are symptomatic of living in a culture that places high-value on masculine traits. Until we bring a feminist consciousness to our business development, we will unwittingly embed these patriarchal values into the foundation of our enterprise, thus reaffirming and recreating them.

The first trimester of business development is the *Visioning* stage — a profoundly creative time where you imagine possibilities and connect with your purpose.

It is here that you will dream up an holistic, integrated, grounded, and intentional business that embodies your feminist principles. To skip this powerful phase is folly. Without a deep knowing of *what* you want to create and *why*, you will build a business without a solid, stable root structure. You may even create a company you don't actually want to work in once it's up-and-running. And, over time, you might find that your business behaviors are out of alignment with your own values and beliefs.

Nearly all conventional business development frameworks fixate on *Engineering* and *Actualization*, taking the *Conception* and *Visioning* stages for granted. The result is a glut of masculinist businesses that run like well-oiled machines but lack a larger vision and a deeper sense of purpose. The Trimester Theory offers us another way — one that brings feminine principles to the fore.

We need more visionaries and more visionary businesses. The only way this will happen is if we spend more time cultivating and honing our visions. My goal with this Handbook is to encourage you to s-l-o-w d-o-w-n and honor the invisible, imaginative stages of the business birthing process before diving into *doing*.

Creating a new human takes nine months. Even if you're very impatient, it still takes nine months. To bring a new enterprise into the world — one that embodies your values and puts your feminist principles into practice — will likely take you somewhere between nine months and three years. It might take you a whole lifetime. It doesn't really matter.

If you are brand new to business and feeling both excited and overwhelmed, this Handbook will help you take your first steps. If you are already in the process of birthing your business and have gotten lost or ahead of yourself, it will guide you gently back to where you belong. Locating where you are in the process will point you to your tasks at hand and reduce frustration.

As you get the hang of it, you'll quickly discover the Trimester Theory isn't just for beginners. Once you know the stages, you will cycle through them again and again as you grow your business. You'll learn when it's time to focus on your pleasures and make fertile space to conceive something new. You'll develop the habit of cultivating a vision before rushing in to engineer a solution. As you innovate new products, hire employees, rebrand your business, and design your strategic plan, you can rely on the Trimester Theory to provide guidance, support, and reassurance for your process.

To benefit from this book you don't need to have children or a womb. You don't need to be able to get pregnant or even want to have kids. You don't have to identify as a woman or a mother. The Trimester Theory uses the stages of prenatal development as a template for bringing your business to life. You already have first-hand knowledge of this process because you went through it yourself, in utero!

Transforming a business from idea to reality is a special time, one you can't get back once your business is up-and-running. Pregnancy and parenting are two distinctly different projects. The gestational period is full of feelings, fears, potential, and possibilities. It offers you the unique opportunity to clarify your purpose, reconnect with your passions, prioritize your pleasures, lead with your values, and step into your personal power.

As you embark upon this entrepreneurial journey, allow the stages to support you in becoming more integrated, embodied, and committed to your calling. Let the process surprise and delight you. Allow your work to become play. Shed whatever you are ready to let go of. Remember the parts of yourself you want to reclaim. Let yourself be transformed by this process.

LET
YOUR
BUSINESS
BIRTH
YOU

HOW TO USE THIS HANDBOOK

Start by reading through the entire Handbook so that you grasp the arc, then go back and spend more time in the phase you're currently working through. Engage with the questions. Read them through a few times and pull out the ones that feel juiciest. Get out your journal and do some writing. Or, don't write anything at all. You could lie down and just imagine. Or, make diagrams, paint your vision, set up spreadsheets, write lists, draw a mind map. Get your ideas out of your body in a way that is fun for you. Play with the themes and questions of your phase in a creative, material way.

As you read through the trimesters, you will likely see yourself in more than one phase. This is because we run the gestation cycle over and over. In the process of bringing your business to life, you will be following this sequence for the development of the individual parts, such as making a new website, developing a new product, hiring an employee, and so on. However, you will only be in one phase at a time for the overall development of your new business.

BE HONEST with yourself in identifying which stage you are in right now. Use the questions at the end of each section as a test. For example, *Can you see your business clearly in your mind's eye and describe it easily to others? Is your vision written down?* If not, you are in the *Conception* or *Visioning* stage. Don't move ahead until you have completed the primary tasks for your phase. Remember — this isn't a race. Rushing ahead will only imperil your business and waste your precious time and money.

This Handbook is meant to be one tool in your business development toolbox. I provide you with an overarching framework, but it is up to you to seek out books, mentors, conversations, solutions, and ideas relevant to your industry and in alignment with your values. Harness your curiosity and inner explorer to gather additional resources for your stage.

If you have friends or collaborators who are also entering into entrepreneurship, I recommend forming a book group or happy hour crew to share your insights and support each other in the birthing processes. The questions herein provide you with rich discussion prompts to guide your conversations.

Whether you are birthing a new business, or a new way of being in business, the Trimester Theory will assist you in accessing a deeper level of purpose, pleasure, and integration, and help you lay a strong foundation for your radiant and radical business.

YOU ARE NOT YOUR BUSINESS

YOUR BUSINESS IS NOT YOU

YOU ARE NOT YOUR BUSINESS

Your business has its own distinct identity, its own unique spirit. You are not your business. Your business is not you. You are *in a relationship* with your business. At the beginning of any new enterprise, when you are bringing your vision to life, this dynamic generally resembles a parent-child relationship.

Your business has chosen you inasmuch as you have chosen it. Your business wants to be born, to live in the world. It has a mission to fulfill and it has chosen you *(yes, you!)* as its steward. Your business offers you the opportunity to enliven your purpose. It has the power to infuse your life with abundance, pleasure, and play. It will show you where you need to grow, helping you become more integrated and empowered. It will also bring you to your knees. I don't know a single entrepreneur who hasn't found herself curled up and sobbing in the fetal position at some point in the birthing process. When it happens to you, know that you are on the path.

Your business has its own unique spirit with its own distinct personality and purpose. Sometimes its needs will align with yours, other times they will be in tension. Your relationship will change over time, as you grow and evolve. Eventually, with proper parenting, your business will walk and talk and feed itself and (hopefully*!*) make money for you while you're asleep.

As in parenthood, when you commit to bringing your business into the world, you become responsible for nurturing its wellbeing and helping it become self-sufficient. Over time, you and your business will become a team, a collaborative partnership. But in your first 3 to 5 years in business you fill a parental role — guiding, tending, feeding, teaching, loving, forgiving, fretting, enforcing, cleaning up messes, and generally being the adult in the room (even when you don't feel like it).

Understanding your business as an entity separate from yourself is imperative to the success of your endeavor and crucial to your own health and wellbeing. *Why?* Let's revisit the child metaphor.

What happens if, as a parent, you do not cultivate your child's independence? It will be very difficult for both of you to mature. As an entrepreneur, you will likely invest your happiness and self-esteem in the performance of your business. Without healthy boundaries, it will also be very hard to relax. You will probably never feel like you're not working. You run the risk of internalizing failures or mistakes. You will build resentments and, eventually, burn out. Your business will be stifled and may fail financially. And, you will miss opportunities to learn, play, grow, and experiment because you are too busy controlling everything.

Just like birthing a baby, birthing your business is largely the work of getting it out of your body. The work of the new entrepreneur is learning to discern yourself from your business. In the beginning, your business will exist solely in your mind's eye. As you progress through the stages, you do the labor of materializing your business outside of your body through your writings, drawings, sketches, blueprints, plans, designs, operations manuals, financial spreadsheets, legal paperwork, office furniture, website, business bank account, employee handbook, and so on. Until, finally, it is fully formed and open for business.

Treat the gestational process with reverence and play. Procure a beautiful journal to capture your vision, stock up on your favorite colored pens, set up your computer docs with your favorite font. Getting your business out of your body doesn't have to be boring or joyless. Bring your business into the world with the same creative spirit you wish to inhabit once it's up-and-running.

As you move the business out of your body, it will take on its own identity and claim its place in the world. It will also gain the ability to grow, flourish, and function without your constant supervision. You, then, are freed up to have a life beyond work and a business that you love instead of resent.

Remember — you are not your business and your business is not you. You are *in a relationship*. So, what kind of relationship do you want to be in?

THE GESTATIONAL STAGES

BE
THE
OVUM
NOT
THE
SPERM

CONCEPTION

Making a new human begins with conception: sperm fertilizes egg. For entrepreneurs, you gain the deep knowing that you want to bring a business into the world, although you might not yet know exactly what. In creative terms, you conceive of an idea. For some people, this inspiration spark is immediately accompanied by a vision. Others experience a powerful desire to bring a business forth but a lack of clarity around what it will be.

Conception is the most powerful of all the stages. This is the place of *ALL POSSIBILITIES*. Here, you sit in the soil, gaze at your field, and imagine what you will plant, lovingly tend, and eventually harvest. This phase is all about *fertility*. Think of the uterine lining, rich with nourishment to sustain life, waiting for a fertilized seed to implant. Once you acclimate to the openness, the quiet, the darkness, and the dirt, you realize this is a place of profound potential.

The womb is the sacred internal place that nurtures new life. The *Conception* phase asks you to cultivate your receptivity — to go within, learn the voice of your intuition and inner wisdom, connect with your deep needs and desires, reclaim your personal power, and awaken to your life's purpose.

The key that unlocks your fertility is: *pleasure.*

The work of this phase is to explore what feels good and reconnect with the things that bring you joy. This is the time to delight in your creativity, playfulness, sensuality, and magic. Practice trusting yourself and letting your intuition guide you. Cultivate a deeper authority over your life. Attune to the needs of your physical body. Connect with the natural world. Nurture. Nourish. Let go of the things that don't serve you (or your business). Heal your forgotten, neglected, and disparate parts. Embrace opportunities to become more integrated, embodied, conscious, connected, and empowered.

The *Conception* stage speaks the language of synchronicity, coincidence, and subtle messages. When you are in fertile flow, you are tapped into Universal Consciousness. There is no efforting here, nothing to *do* — conception is a spontaneous event. Release the need to problem solve or "figure out" your business.

Be the ovum, not the sperm.
Let your business choose you.

Redirect your focus towards your pleasures, again and again. Trust that what you're good at and what you enjoy are such because that's what you're supposed to do more of. Your pleasures will point you to your purpose.

In this stage you will awaken to your calling, the *why* of your enterprise—your mission. Your concept will likely be very granular. You may grasp three or four constituent parts that will become your business. Think of these as *seeds* or *elementals*. Let them tell you what they want to become.

YOU WILL KNOW THIS PHASE IS COMPLETE WHEN—
- You feel fully committed to and totally in love with your business idea or concept.
- You can articulate your purpose and the elementals of your business.

CORRESPONDING ARCHETYPES—
The Fool, High Priestess, Empress

QUESTIONS FOR THOSE WANTING TO CONCEIVE

WHAT IS YOUR CONCEPTION STYLE?

ARE YOU LOVEMAKING?

ARE YOU TAKING A CLINICAL APPROACH?

ARE YOU RUSHING OR FORCING A TIMELINE?

ARE YOU SPENDING ALL OF YOUR TIME IN YOUR BRAIN, TRYING TO "FIGURE IT OUT"?

ARE YOU ENJOYING & NURTURING YOUR BODY?

HOW CAN YOU CULTIVATE MORE SENSUAL PLEASURE, DISCOVERY, & DELIGHT?

~~~~~~

WHEN DO YOU FEEL MOST ALIVE?

WHAT BRINGS YOU DEEP PLEASURE?

WHICH PEOPLE, PLACES, PLANTS, SCENTS, FOODS, STORIES, & IMAGES ENERGIZE YOU?

WHICH DRAIN OR DEPLETE YOU?

ARE YOU CONNECTING DAILY WITH THE THINGS THAT BRING YOU JOY?

WHICH HAS MORE WEIGHT IN YOUR
DECISION-MAKING: YOUR INTELLECT
OR YOUR INTUITION?

HOW OFTEN DO YOU FOLLOW
YOUR INSTINCTS?

DO YOU REGULARLY LOOK
TO OTHERS FOR ANSWERS?

WHAT DOES YOUR INTUITION FEEL LIKE?
WHERE DO YOU FEEL IT IN YOUR BODY?

HOW WOULD YOUR LIFE CHANGE IF
YOU TRUSTED YOURSELF MORE DEEPLY?

WHAT ARE YOUR FEELINGS
ABOUT PARENTHOOD?

WHAT DO YOU ADMIRE IN YOUR MOTHER?
HOW DID YOUR MOTHER FAIL YOU?

WHAT DO YOU ADMIRE IN YOUR FATHER?
HOW DID YOUR FATHER FAIL YOU?

WHAT STRENGTHS HAVE YOU INHERITED?

WHAT ANCESTRAL PATTERNS DO YOU
WANT TO LEAVE BEHIND?

WHAT FAMILIAL WOUNDS ARE YOU
READY TO HEAL?

WHAT DOES "BEING A GOOD
ANCESTOR" MEAN TO YOU?

WHERE IS THE PLACE YOU
FEEL MOST LIKE YOURSELF?

HOW CAN YOU CONNECT WITH
THAT FEELING, DAILY?

ARE YOU SPENDING TIME WITH NATURE?

ARE YOU NOURISHING THE PLANTS
AND ANIMALS AROUND YOU?

ARE YOU NOURISHING YOURSELF?

HOW CAN YOU CREATE MORE SPACE IN
YOUR LIFE TO RECEIVE NOURISHMENT?

WHERE DO YOU NEED TO CREATE SPACE TO
RECEIVE MORE NOURISHMENT IN YOUR BODY?

DO YOU SLEEP WHEN YOU'RE TIRED, EAT WHEN YOU'RE HUNGRY, PEE WHEN YOU NEED TO?

HOW CAN YOU BECOME MORE PRESENT IN THE LOWER HALF OF YOUR BODY, ESPECIALLY YOUR SECOND CHAKRA/PELVIC BOWL?

DOES YOUR BODY TELL YOU WHAT IT NEEDS?

HOW DO YOU USUALLY RESPOND?

ARE YOU TENDING TO YOUR SPIRITUAL AND EMOTIONAL NEEDS?

IS THERE ANYONE YOU NEED TO FORGIVE, INCLUDING YOURSELF?

HOW CAN YOU CULTIVATE MORE COMPASSION & NURTURANCE TOWARDS YOURSELF?

WHAT FASCINATES YOU?

WHAT IGNITES YOUR PASSIONS?

WHAT DO YOU LOVE?

WHAT ARE THE NEEDS
OF YOUR BODY?

WHAT DO YOU FEEL CALLED
TO CREATE?

WHAT NEEDS HEALING?

WHAT DO YOU WANT
TO INNOVATE?

WHAT CHANGE DO YOU
WISH TO SPARK?

WHAT DO YOU LONG FOR
THAT DOESN'T EXIST?

WHAT COULD A BUSINESS LOOK LIKE THAT INTEGRATES *ALL* OF THESE?

ACTIVITIES TO SUPPORT CONCEPTION

TAKE A RELAXING BATH.
ADD A CUP OF EPSOM SALTS & SOME LAVENDER OIL. LIGHT CANDLES. DO NOT BRING ANYTHING INTO THE BATH WITH YOU. SPEND AT LEAST 20 MINUTES SOAKING.

SENSUAL SEX.
WITH YOURSELF OR A BELOVED.

FEEL INTO YOUR BODY.
SPEND 10 MINUTES LYING ON YOUR BACK WITH YOUR EYES CLOSED. SET A TIMER. FOCUS ON YOUR BREATH. NOTICE THE SENSATIONS & COLORS THAT APPEAR AS YOU BECOME MORE PRESENT IN YOUR BODY.

ADOPT A PRACTICE OF WRITING OR DANCING
20 MINUTES, FIRST THING IN THE MORNING.

GO ON A NATURE DATE.
SPEND QUIET TIME CONNECTING WITH MAMA EARTH. TOUCH THE PLANTS. LISTEN CAREFULLY. CELEBRATE HER BEAUTY.

TAKE A SOCIAL MEDIA SABBATICAL.

EAT MINDFULLY.
NOTICE SMELLS, COLORS, TASTES, AND THE FEEL OF WHAT YOU'RE EATING. CHEW SLOWLY TO TASTE EACH BITE.

NAP.

YOUR
PLEASURES
WILL
POINT YOU
TO
YOUR
PURPOSE

DREAMING IS A FORM OF PLANNING

—GLORIA STEINEM

THE VISIONING STAGE
FIRST TRIMESTER

In the first trimester of human development, cells start the process of rapidly multiplying and organizing themselves into human form. In this embryonic stage, all the raw materials needed to create a new life (the chromosomes) are present.

This is the *Visioning* phase — the ideating stage, where you will cycle through myriad possibilities of what your business could be until you gain clarity on what you want to create. Once *Conception* has taken place, you begin fleshing out your concept. This is the phase of *incubation* and *imagination* — a time for curiosity, daydreams, and creativity. As ideas arrive, you will discern which feel good to you, align with your values, and energize your vision, and which are depleting or distract from your purpose.

Your guiding questions are, **What does my business look like? What could it be?**

Visioning is the artist's realm. Here, inspiration will move through you, wanting to be expressed in visible form. This is not the time for problem solving, perfectionism, or practicalities. Dancing between the realm of the imaginary and the tangible, your work is to capture ideas as they arrive. You begin giving form to your business through language and imagery.

Like *Conception*, this stage requires you to tend to the health of your receptivity. You must cultivate space (in your body, in your life) for ideas to arrive. Set aside time for creative play. Build collage boards, make mind maps, sketch design ideas, draw up colorful lists so you can *see* your business more clearly. Gather colored pens and carry a journal with you to capture information as it comes through.

In the early weeks (or months) of *Visioning*, stay very open to keep the inspiration flowing. Don't get attached to your first idea. Your vision will shift and evolve several times before it settles. This is a good thing; it indicates you are *choosing* the right business for you and creating with intention.

Some business beginners get ahead of themselves in this stage. In their excitement to make their vision real, they invest in websites, logos, or business cards. Remember — your business is still taking form. Use creative processes to help you find clarity but avoid spending big dollars on branding or marketing until the *Actualization* stage.

As you move through *Visioning*, your task will transform from ideating to editing. Use your core values and discernment to guide you as you hone your vision. Some ideas will come to you that don't align with your beliefs. Others simply won't be financially viable. A vision may arrive that feeds your ego but doesn't nourish your soul. Use your intuition and feel into your body to determine what's in alignment with you and your purpose. Take ownership of your beliefs and accept accountability for the business you will create.

Many people choose to keep their pregnancy private until the second trimester when the fetus's viability is assured. Guard your energetic boundaries and reveal your vision only to those you trust. Your nascent business is fragile and vulnerable to criticism and sabotage. Hold your magic close.

By the end of this phase, you will either commit to shepherding your business vision into the world or you will abort. You may decide that entrepreneurship isn't for you, and that's all right.

YOU WILL KNOW THIS PHASE IS COMPLETE WHEN —
- You can see your business clearly in your mind's eye and describe it easily to others.
- The vision is out of your body and onto paper (either written, typed, drawn, or mapped).
- You don't know how it works yet, and that's okay*!*

CORRESPONDING ARCHETYPES —
Visionary, Alchemist, Artist, Dreamer, Magician

WHEN DO YOUR BEST IDEAS COME TO YOU?

WHEN ARE YOU AT YOUR
MOST VISIONARY?

QUESTIONS FOR CULTIVATING A VISION

DO YOU FEEL MOST COMFORTABLE
EXPRESSING YOURSELF THROUGH WORDS,
IMAGES, COLORS, CHARTS, OR SOUNDS?
ANOTHER MEDIUM?

DO YOU DEVOTE TIME DAILY TO YOUR
CREATIVE PRACTICE?

DO YOU IDENTIFY AS AN ARTIST?

THINK BACK ON SOME OF YOUR FAVORITE
CREATIONS—WHAT CONDITIONS
NURTURED YOUR PROCESS?

DO YOU HAVE BASIC SUPPLIES ON-HAND
TO EXPRESS YOUR VISION: PAPER, PENS,
MARKERS, GLITTER, AND SO ON?

DO YOU HAVE INSPIRING IDEAS,
WORDS, AND IMAGES IN YOUR
WORKING & LIVING SPACES?

HOW CAN YOU BRING MORE INSPIRATION
INTO YOUR PHYSICAL REALM?

WHEN ARE YOU MOST TAPPED
INTO CREATIVE FLOW?

WHEN DO YOU EXPRESS YOURSELF
WITHOUT CENSURE?

WHAT PEOPLE, IDEAS, IMAGES, PLACES,
& THINGS SPARK YOUR CREATIVITY?

WHAT DOES THE VOICE OF
YOUR CRITIC SOUND LIKE?
WHOSE VOICE IS THIS?

WHAT ARE THE WAYS IN WHICH YOU
ARE DENYING YOURSELF WHAT YOU
DEEPLY WANT?

ARE YOU SHRINKING YOURSELF OR
YOUR VISION BASED ON INHERITED OR
EXTERNAL IDEAS OF WHAT'S NORMAL,
REASONABLE, OR REALISTIC?

WHAT DO YOU NEED IN ORDER TO
BEGIN LIVING AND WORKING BY
YOUR OWN RULES?

WHAT BRINGS YOU DEEP PLEASURE?

WHAT ARE YOUR PERSISTENT PASSIONS?

WHAT ARE YOUR CORE VALUES?

WHAT IS YOUR LIFE'S PURPOSE?

WHAT IS YOUR DEFINITION OF SUCCESS?

WHAT DO YOU FEEL CALLED TO CREATE?

WHO MIGHT OFFER INSIGHTS, IDEAS, WISDOM, AND SUPPORT FOR YOUR VISION?

WHO DO YOU WANT TO COLLABORATE WITH?

CAN YOU SET UP A MEETING WITH THEM?

WHAT DOES YOUR BUSINESS LOOK LIKE IN
1 YEAR?
3 YEARS?
5 YEARS?

WHAT DOES YOUR LIFE LOOK LIKE IN 1 YEAR?
3 YEARS?
5 YEARS?

IF YOU HAD THE RESOURCES TO MAKE YOUR BUSINESS EVERYTHING YOU DREAM & DESIRE, WHAT COULD IT BE?

EMBODY YOUR FEMINIST PRINCIPLES IN YOUR BUSINESS PRACTICES

THE ENGINEERING STAGE
SECOND TRIMESTER

In the second trimester, the fetus takes on recognizable human form. Bones and skeleton start to develop, providing structure. Organs arrange themselves and gain functionality. Fingerprints become evident.

With a clear vision of your business, you transition out of the creative ideation of the *Visioning* stage and enter into *Engineering*. Here you draw up plans and blueprints, tending to the practical matters of *how* your business will function. This phase is filled with research, learning, exploration, problem-solving, and decision-making as you lay the groundwork for your healthy enterprise. If the first trimester is the stage of *imagination*, the second trimester is the stage of *innovation*.

The guiding question here is, **How does it work?**

In this stage, you develop the fundamental structural supports of your business — write your business plan, finalize your budget, secure funding, register your business, acquire any necessary licenses or regulatory certifications, create financial forecasts, clarify your core offer, develop your operating procedures, and so on. Think: outlines and spreadsheets, systems and structures, operations and mechanics.

You don't need to be an expert on business before you begin *Engineering*. You will learn as you go. If you are brand new to entrepreneurship, this is the time to draw on the wisdom of those who have gone before you. *What choices did they make and why?* Devour books and articles, meet with business mentors, take classes, think collaboratively with colleagues, host a co-learning happy hour with your business babes. Get practiced asking for help and admitting when you don't know.

Importantly, this is also where you choose how to embody your feminist principles in your business practices. Gather as much information as you can about different ways of doing business. As you develop familiarity with different business models, you'll begin to devise your own.

Look for existing solutions that allow you to work with greater ease. Invest in programs, apps, platforms, and out-of-the-box systems that will increase your flow and decrease your stress. When needed, redesign others' systems to bring them into alignment with your values.

Some artists and solopreneurs will want to skip this stage, seeing it as boring, mechanical, or uncreative. However, without an infrastructure, your business will not function without you there, and you will be unable to grow your company without significantly increasing your workload, which will eventually lead to burnout. Creating clear and consistent systems provides stability for you and your company. Devise procedures and protocols so that your business is less reliant on you and your body. This will help you work with more ease and joy, and allow you increased creative capacity in the long run as your business develops its independence.

In *Engineering*, you will naturally become more public with your business idea, sharing it with others as you seek wisdom and resources. Begin cultivating community around your vision. Gather your team of advisors, consultants, contractors, employees, vendors, colleagues, and collaborators (don't forget your healers and therapists!). These are people you can call on to support you. Their enthusiasm and energy will carry you through the intensive labor of the *Actualization* stage.

YOU WILL KNOW THIS PHASE IS COMPLETE WHEN —
- Your business systems and structures are committed to paper (or pixels).
- Anyone who looks at your collection of documents, drawings, and spreadsheets will easily understand what your business is and how it works.
- You feel grounded and supported because you understand the structural pillars and financial flow that will provide stability in your business and enable it to thrive.

CORRESPONDING ARCHETYPES —
Architect, Engineer, Inventor, Student

QUESTIONS FOR ENGINEERING

HOW CAN YOU WORK MORE COLLABORATIVELY?

HAVE YOU REACHED OUT TO BUSINESS MENTORS & LOCAL ORGANIZATIONS THAT OFFER FREE GUIDANCE AND SUPPORT?

ARE YOU DROWNING IN OVERWHELM & THE FEELING THAT YOU DON'T KNOW WHAT YOU'RE DOING?

ARE YOU ACCESSING THE WISDOM AND EXPERTISE OF THOSE WHO HAVE GONE BEFORE YOU?

ARE YOU TAKING CLASSES?

ARE YOU USING THE LIBRARY?

ARE YOU ASKING FOR HELP?

ARE YOU FEELING CHAOTIC?
IS ORGANIZATION A PROBLEM?

ARE YOU TRYING TO REINVENT THE WHEEL?

WHAT EXISTING SOLUTIONS (SYSTEMS, TOOLS, & TECHNOLOGIES) CAN YOU IMPLEMENT TO CREATE MORE EASE?

WHAT ARE YOUR FEMINIST PRINCIPLES & BELIEFS?

HOW WILL YOU BRING THESE INTO YOUR BUSINESS PRACTICES?

WHAT DO YOU WANT TO DO DIFFERENTLY THAN OTHERS, NOT BUSINESS-AS-USUAL?

WHAT NEW PRACTICES DO YOU WANT TO INNOVATE?

ARE YOU EMBODYING YOUR VALUES IN YOUR SYSTEMS & STRUCTURES?

ARE YOU APPROACHING BUSINESS AS ART?

WHAT KIND OF RELATIONSHIP
DO YOU HAVE WITH MONEY?

WHAT KIND OF RELATIONSHIP
DO YOU WANT TO HAVE WITH MONEY?

HOW DOES YOUR BODY FEEL WHEN YOU ARE
TENDING TO YOUR FINANCES (OR EVEN JUST
THINKING ABOUT MONEY)?

HAVE YOU DONE YOUR FINANCIAL DUE
DILIGENCE SO YOU KNOW YOU ARE CREATING A
HEALTHY BUSINESS, NOT AN EXPENSIVE HOBBY?

HOW CAN YOU CULTIVATE MORE EASE
AND CONFIDENCE AROUND MONEY?

ARE YOU NURTURING AND
CARING FOR YOUR BODY?

ARE YOU TAKING TIME
FOR REST AND PLAY?

IF YOU ARE FEELING STUCK, LOST, FRUSTRATED, OR OVERWHELMED, HOME IN ON WHAT'S MISSING—

DO YOU NEED MORE INFORMATION?

DO YOU NEED TO BE PATIENT?

ARE YOU FORGETTING YOUR RESOURCES?

HAS SOMEONE ELSE ALREADY SOLVED THIS PROBLEM?

DO YOU NEED REST?

DO YOU NEED PLAY?

DO YOU NEED A BREAK?

DO YOU NEED HELP?

YOUR FEELINGS POINT YOU TO YOUR NEEDS.

TAKE THE TIME TO IDENTIFY YOUR FEELINGS & LISTEN TO THEIR GUIDANCE.

WHAT IS OUT OF ALIGNMENT—

IN YOUR BODY?

IN YOUR LIFE?

IN YOUR RELATIONSHIP
WITH MONEY?

IN YOUR RELATIONSHIP
WITH OTHERS?

IN YOUR COMMUNITY?

WITH THE EARTH?

WHERE ARE THERE DISCONNECTS
BETWEEN WHAT YOU
BELIEVE AND WHAT YOU DO?

HOW CAN YOUR BUSINESS BE A HEALING FOR YOURSELF & OTHERS?

BREATHE

THE ACTUALIZATION STAGE
THIRD TRIMESTER

In the third trimester, the fetus becomes fully viable: the bones are developed, its eyes can open, it practices breathing in-utero, and it gains weight rapidly. The culmination of the third trimester is the hard work of labor and, eventually, birth.

This is the *Actualization* stage, where you implement your plans and prepare to launch your business into the world. This stage is marked by physicality—*doing* and *details*. Most of the high-level, creative imagining and strategic planning has already occurred. Here you are engaged with the physical *labor* of carrying out your plans.

You tend to the material needs of your business— securing and configuring your physical and digital spaces, buying supplies, hiring people, getting business cards, designing a website, running errands (so many errands*!*), coordinating vendors, testing your systems, and getting all the "things" up-and-running so that your business can thrive as it launches into the world.

In *Actualization* you confront the physical realities of money, time, energy, health, resources, people, regulations, commerce, and Capitalism. You must learn to work creatively with constraints. Some of your best laid plans will need to be modified or jettisoned. Reduce your stress and suffering by letting go of attachment to your perfect vision and watertight engineering. Running a business requires constant adaptation. Start practicing this now.

Like the *Visioning* stage, *Actualization* invites alchemy. In *Visioning*, you are co-creating with spirit, in *Actualization* you are co-creating with your bank account, zoning regulators, vendors, landlords, contractors, designers, new hires, technology, and the like. Cultivate cooperation and collaboration instead of being a tiny tyrant and demanding your way.

The more you are able to ask for support, stay grounded, and trust that your needs will be met, the less taxing this phase will be. Tending to the basic requirements of your body (food, rest, sleep, exercise, social connection, touch, spiritual grounding) will support you during this time of high-output labor.

Your guiding words here are *resiliency* and *resourcefulness*. You will likely feel moments of profound despair or defeat. You may experience exhaustion, overwhelm, terror, and elation. Possibly all at once. It can be helpful to remember times in the past that you succeeded in the face of adversity, improvised clever solutions to difficult problems, or when someone miraculously showed up at just the right moment with exactly what you needed. Invite synergy, spirit, and magic to support you through this stage.

Your limits *will* be tested — do not sabotage yourself or your business. Labor is a temporary state, a means to an end. Reconnect with your vision and call on friends when you feel lost or demoralized. As anyone who's naturally birthed a child will tell you: *breathe through it.*

As this stage proceeds, your business will look and feel real, because it is*!*

YOU WILL KNOW THIS PHASE IS COMPLETE WHEN —
- You open your doors for business.

CORRESPONDING ARCHETYPES —
Athlete, Magician, Charioteer, Warrior, Laborer

WHAT DO YOU NEED, RIGHT NOW?

HOW DO YOU TREAT YOURSELF IN TIMES OF EXTREME BUSYNESS AND STRESS?

HOW DO YOU TREAT OTHERS?

CAN YOU DEVELOP A DEEPER PRACTICE OF TELLING THE TRUTH & ASKING FOR WHAT YOU NEED?

WHAT WOULD THAT LOOK LIKE?

QUESTIONS FOR ACTUALIZATION

HOW ARE YOU TREATING YOUR BODY?

ARE YOU NOURISHING YOURSELF?

WHAT ARE YOU NEGLECTING?

WHAT WILL SUPPORT YOU IN PRIORITIZING THE NEEDS OF YOUR BODY?

WHAT DO YOU NEED, RIGHT NOW?

HOW CAN YOU MEET THIS NEED, TO THE BEST OF YOUR ABILITY?

WHAT ARE YOU GRATEFUL FOR?

WHAT CHOICES ARE YOU
MAKING WITH YOUR MONEY?

ARE THESE CHOICES IN ALIGNMENT
WITH YOUR VALUES?

ARE YOU DEVELOPING HABITS AND PRACTICES
NOW THAT YOU WANT TO CARRY INTO THE
RUNNING OF YOUR BUSINESS?

IF NOT, WHAT NEEDS TO CHANGE?

WHAT PART OF YOUR VISION OR PLAN ARE YOU ATTACHED TO THAT IS CAUSING YOU SUFFERING?

WHERE ARE YOU HAVING TO COMPROMISE YOUR VALUES?

IS THERE AN INNOVATIVE SOLUTION IN ALIGNMENT WITH YOUR VALUES THAT YOU HAVEN'T CONSIDERED YET?

IF YOU CAN'T IMAGINE A SOLUTION THAT EMBODIES YOUR VALUES RIGHT NOW, CAN YOU ENVISION A SOLUTION IN 1 YEAR? 5 YEARS? 20 YEARS?

CAN YOU MAKE COMPROMISES AND STILL HAVE INTEGRITY?

DO YOU REMEMBER WHY YOU STARTED THIS?

HOW CAN YOU STAY CONNECTED WITH YOUR PURPOSE?

CAN YOU LET THE SPIRIT OF YOUR BUSINESS GUIDE YOU?

CAN YOU RELAX & RECEIVE?

CAN YOU ALLOW
IT TO COME TO YOU?

CAN YOU LET GO OF
YOUR TIMELINE?

CAN YOU EXPERIENCE THE JOY IN
LETTING PEOPLE HELP YOU?

CAN YOU FEEL WHATEVER YOU'RE
FEELING WITHOUT JUDGEMENT?

CAN YOU TRUST THE PROCESS?

CAN YOU CONNECT WITH THE BEAUTY
OF WHAT YOU'RE CREATING?

CAN YOU TAKE TIME FOR
REST & RECOVERY?

CAN YOU PAUSE TO CELEBRATE
YOUR ACCOMPLISHMENTS,
BIG & SMALL?

CAN YOU LET IT BE EASY?

CONGRATULATIONS

ON YOUR BEAUTIFUL BUSINESS!

NOTES

9 In my first book, *Proposals for the Feminine Economy,* I put forth a vision of a new economic and entrepreneurial paradigm, founded on feminine and feminist principles. I outline the "12 Principles for Prototyping a Feminist Business" as an antidote to the masculine Capitalist economy we live in. Among these Principles are *Let it Be Easy* and *Free Yourself From the Myth of the Meritocracy*.

17 Liliana Barzola of Lotus Lantern Healing Arts first suggested to me that a business is like a child and helped me develop discernment between myself and my business though her spiritual perspective. Using her clairvoyant gifts, she showed me that my business has its own unique spirit, a soul, that I can communicate and co-create with.

19 Nicole Lewis-Keeber brings a therapuetic perspective to business development and introduced me to the idea that I am in a relationship with my business. "What kind of relationship do you want to be in [with your business]?" is informed by her work.

24 Audre Lorde's foundational feminist text, "Uses of the Erotic, the Erotic as Power" from her collection *Sister Outsider* speaks to the centrality of pleasure to the feminist project. Recommended reading.

25 *Your Illustrated Guide to Becoming One with the Universe* by Yumi Sakugawa is an excellent resource for *Conception*. She includes a lesson to "plant strange seeds... and let the universe work its magic."

27 In 2016, I attended a phenomenal art-performance-sacred-ceremony-revolutionary-practice, "Spell to Devour the Patriarchy" led by Amanda Yates Garcia (the Oracle of Los Angeles) at the Women's Center for Creative Work. In addition to spiritual ritual, the event included transformational journaling around motherhood and fatherhood. These questions about how our parents failed us come from her.

32 Thich Nhat Hanh's *How to Eat* is a beautifully concise guide to bringing more mindfulness to your mealtime for the purposes of more deeply nourishing your body and spirit. Recommended reading.

37 "Don't try to create and analyse at the same time. They're different processes." Immaculate Heart College Art Department Rule 8 is valuable in the *Visioning* stage. Ideate, imagine, and entertain all possibilities at the beginning of the phase and only when you are overflowing with ideas, edit down.

46 In the United States, the Small Business Administration, S.C.O.R.E., and Women's Business Centers are useful resources for *Engineering*. They offer free and low-cost classes and mentoring. These organizations are particularly helpful for nuts-and-bolts information such as local regulations and compliance information for your jurisdiction. I have encountered advisors who are visionary and enthusiastic as well as those who are condescending and mansplain-y. I recommend seeking out women mentors and being very clear with them about the kind of information and support you are looking for. In general, expect business-as-usual advice. Use your discernment to glean what's useful and leave the rest behind.

47 In *Proposals for the Feminine Economy,* I dive deeper into the idea of "business as art", which I see being distinctly different from "business as a creative process." Art becomes powerful and profound when something is at stake. As you birth your business consider, *"What's at stake?"*

59 Developing business systems and solutions that embody your values is an ongoing project, not something you'll solve once and be done with. In *Let My People Go Surfing,* Yvon Chouinard describes the decades-long process of effecting meaningful change to Patagonia's supply chain. This is life's work stuff. Take the long view.

BACK COVER "Your body is not a lemon, you are not a machine" is an iconic quote by Ina May Gaskin, a woman who has brought thousands of babies across the threshold, into the world. She is the author of *Spiritual Midwifery*. This is my homage to her important work.

THANK YOU to Amelia Hruby for patience, enthusiasm, and expert editing.

JENNIFER ARMBRUST is the founder and director of Sister, where she runs Feminist Business School and consults with entrepreneurs and executives on bringing feminist principles into their business practices. Her work explores the collisions and collusions of art, business, gender, embodiment, and economics.

She opened her first business, a fine art gallery, at the age of twenty-four in Portland, Oregon. Before founding Sister, she was also founder emeritus and partner in an online arts magazine, managing director of an arts nonprofit, principal of a small interactive design studio, and head of her own creative consultancy.

She holds a degree in Critical Theory from The Evergreen State College with continuing studies in small business administration (Portland Community College), interactive design (Pacific Northwest College of Art), and healing arts (Lotus Lantern Healing Arts). She lives in Carpinteria, California, where she is lovingly devoted to surfing 3-foot right point breaks, while dreaming of the elusive left.

sister

**BRINGING FEMINIST PRINCIPLES
INTO BUSINESS PRACTICES**

Feminist Business School
Corporate Consulting
The Fourth Wave publishing

INTERNET ⟫→ sister.is ←⟪ INSTAGRAM